WILD ABOUT ANIMALS

ELEPHANTS

By Emma Huddleston

Kaleidoscope
Minneapolis, MN

The Quest for Discovery Never Ends

This edition first published in 2020 by Kaleidoscope Publishing, Inc.

*For information regarding permission, write to
Kaleidoscope Publishing, Inc.
6012 Blue Circle Drive
Minnetonka, MN 55343*

*Library of Congress Control Number
2019938834*

*ISBN
978-1-64519-002-8 (library bound)
978-1-64494-244-4 (paperback)
978-1-64519-102-5 (ebook)*

Printed in the United States of America.

Bigfoot lurks within one of the images in this book. It's up to you to find him!

TABLE OF CONTENTS

CHAPTER 1

Gentle Giants

An Asian elephant **roams** across the grassland. She is more than 7 feet (2.1 m) tall. She weighs 8,000 pounds (3,600 kg). Her giant body sways side to side as she walks. Tiny pebbles on the ground bounce with each step.

Elephants are the largest living land animals. But they are gentle. This elephant will not fight unless she has to. Usually her large size keeps her from being attacked.

FUN FACT

Female Asian elephants have long teeth called "tushes" instead of tusks.

Female Asian elephants don't have tusks. Some males don't, either.

The elephant is walking to a watering hole. She is thirsty. She can drink 50 gallons (189 L) of water in one day. A **calf** follows her. She shows it where to go and how to drink. She uses her **trunk** to scoop water into her mouth. The calf splashes her. He wants to play.

Elephants can spray water with their trunks.

The water makes streaks on her gray skin. It mixes with the dust on her back. The dust protects her skin from the sun. She sprays water on the calf with her trunk. They splash each other.

FUN FACT
Mud baths protect elephants from the sun.

WHAT'S THE DIFFERENCE BETWEEN AFRICAN AND ASIAN ELEPHANTS?

African elephants are found all over Africa. Their ears are big with round edges. They are shaped a little like Africa. Almost all African elephants have tusks. Asian elephants are smaller. They live in areas between India and Indonesia. Their ears are smaller. Only some adult males have tusks.

Then the elephant looks for food. Twigs snap under her feet. Her body brushes against trees and bushes. Leaves fall to the ground. She uses her trunk to pick up a berry and eat it. Elephant trunks are **sensitive**. They have flaps at the end. These "fingers" can pick up small objects. Asian elephants have one "finger." African elephants have two. The calf watches her. He tries to pick up a berry. The berry falls to the ground. He is still learning how to control his trunk. Elephant trunks have 100,000 muscles. He tries again. Now he eats a tasty berry, too.

Elephants use their trunks to eat, drink, play, and more.

CHAPTER 2

Most African elephants have long tusks.

Trunk and Tusks

The sun shines on an African grassland. A calf is growing. His trunk is getting stronger as he gets older. Elephants are the only living animals with a long trunk. An elephant can use its trunk in many ways. His mother sprays water on her back for bathing. She blows air out of it to make a trumpet sound.

Her trunk can weigh up to 300 pounds (136 kg). It is very strong. It can lift objects up to twice its size. The young elephant copies her. He tries to pick up a rock. She pats his back with her trunk. She is encouraging him. Elephants use their trunks to show emotion.

VERY SMART

Elephants can solve problems. If their belly itches, they look for a stick. They hold it with their trunk. They use it to scratch their belly. Elephants can recognize themselves in a mirror. The only other animals who can do that are dolphins, great apes, and some birds.

She is hungry. She guides the young elephant to a tree. She shows him how to get food. Two white tusks stick out from her mouth. Tusks are giant teeth. They can grow up to 6 feet (1.8 m) long. Each one can weigh 50 pounds (23 kg). She scrapes her tusks on the tree trunk. Pieces of bark break off. Elephants often favor one tusk over the other. It is like how humans are right-handed or left-handed. Her right tusk is a little smaller and worn down. She uses it more.

FUN FACT

Elephants go through six sets of teeth in their life.

Elephants use their trunks and tusks for eating.

PARTS OF AN AFRICAN ELEPHANT

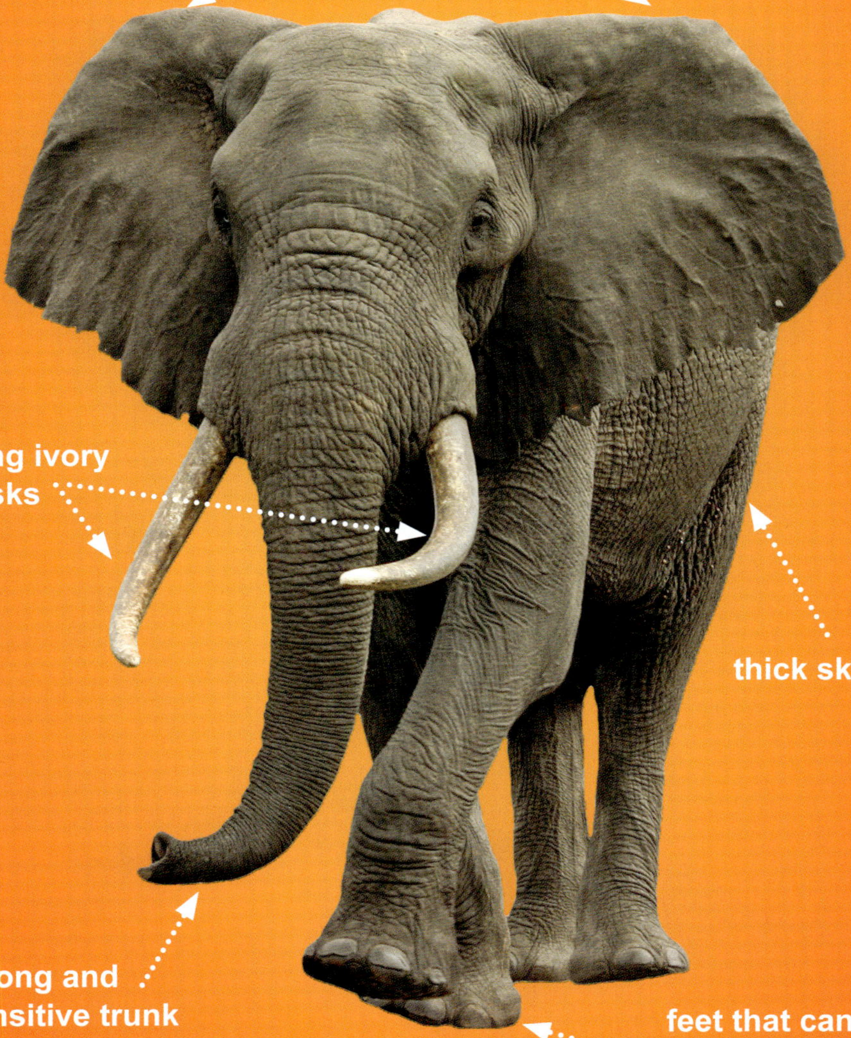

She waves her trunk at another elephant. It is walking toward her. The other elephant comes closer. It is her sister. They wrap their trunks together. They are showing love. Elephants care about one another. They live together in big families. A whole family of elephants will walk slowly if one of them is hurt.

Elephants use their trunks to show emotion.

CHAPTER 3

Family Life

An African elephant roams from place to place. His feet pound the ground. Grass and twigs are crushed. Male elephants usually live alone. Sometimes they form small groups. The oldest and biggest are the leaders. This elephant is only eighteen years old. He just left his mother five years ago. He travels from family to family. Now he is looking to start his own family.

Male elephants are usually solitary, but females create groups.

Water rushes down a nearby river. A female elephant puts one foot in. She is leading her family across. A family of elephants is made of females and calves. It can have up to twenty-five members. Water rushes up her legs. She keeps going.

She is the oldest female in the family. Elephants can live more than sixty years. She is the leader. She protects and guides younger elephants. A calf slips on a rock. She catches it with her trunk. She puts it back on the rock. The family crosses the river. The adults take care of the calves together.

She knows where to lead them for food and water. An elephant's territory can be between 4 and 27 square miles (10 and 70 sq km). They have a strong memory. They can remember where to find watering holes from past journeys.

HOW BIG ARE ELEPHANTS?

Asian Elephant

Elephants can grow more than 9 FEET (2.7 M) tall!

ELEPHANT HERDS

Elephant herds form when more than one family comes together. They might live in the same area. They might drink from the same watering hole. Sometimes families in herds are related. Sometimes they are not. Herds can have up to 1,000 elephants.

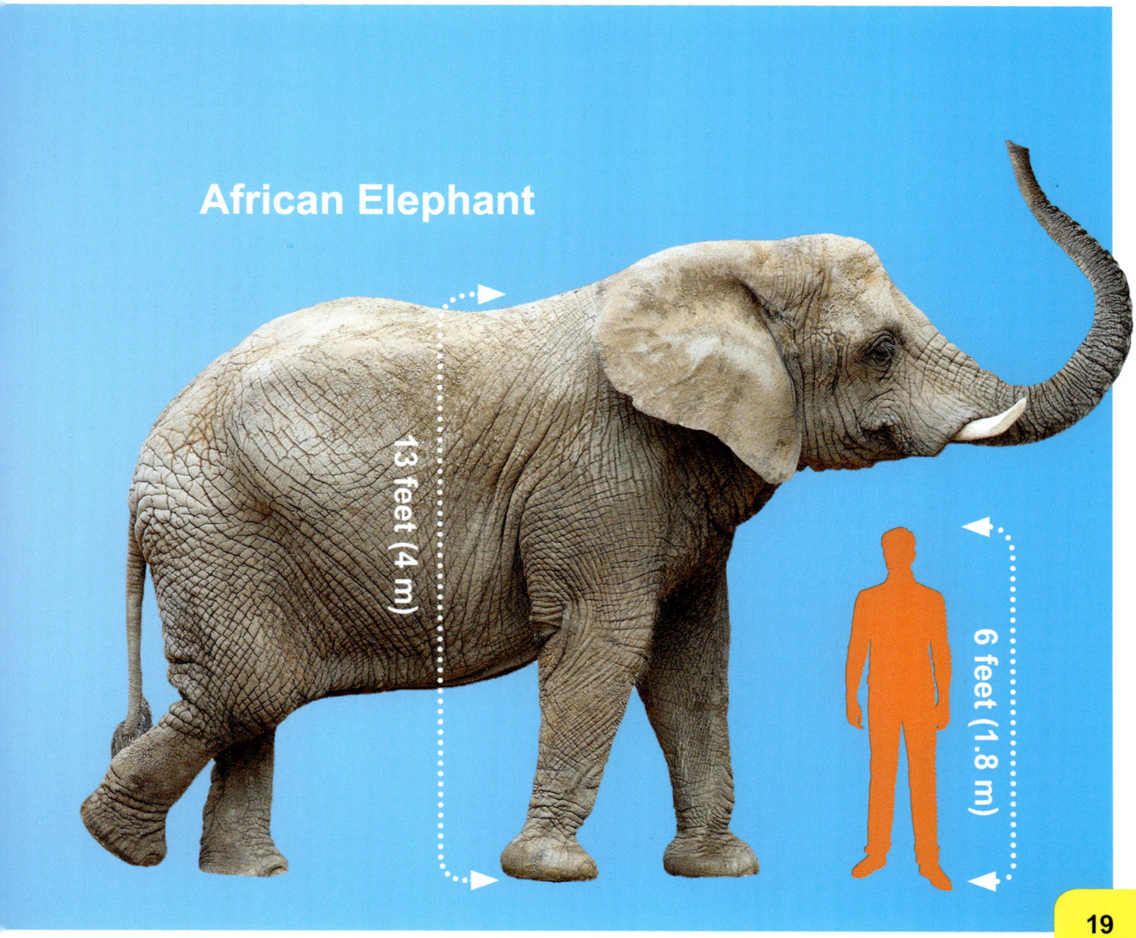

A family gathers around one female. She is giving birth. She makes a trumpet sound. The calf falls to the ground. It is a girl. Adult females give birth to one calf every four or five years. The calf stays with her mother for several years. She learns how to use her trunk. She stumbles when she walks. She likes to play in the mud. Sometimes she gets stuck. Her mother comes to the rescue. They wrap their trunks together. Her mother pulls her out. She is covered in sticky, brown mud.

Baby elephants weigh 200 pounds (91 kg) when they're born!

FUN FACT

Elephants are pregnant for twenty-two months.

CHAPTER 4

Conservation centers help elephants that are sick or injured.

Protecting Elephants

Khun works at an elephant conservation center. It's in Thailand. Someone brought a calf to the center. His mother just died. She was very sick. She had been mistreated by other people. Khun felt bad. The calf was only four months old. She rubbed her hand on his body. Khun took care of the calf for several months. She held a big bottle up to his mouth. Milk dripped down his chin. He was messy.

FUN FACT

People started taming Asian elephants more than 4,000 years ago.

Where Do Elephants Live?

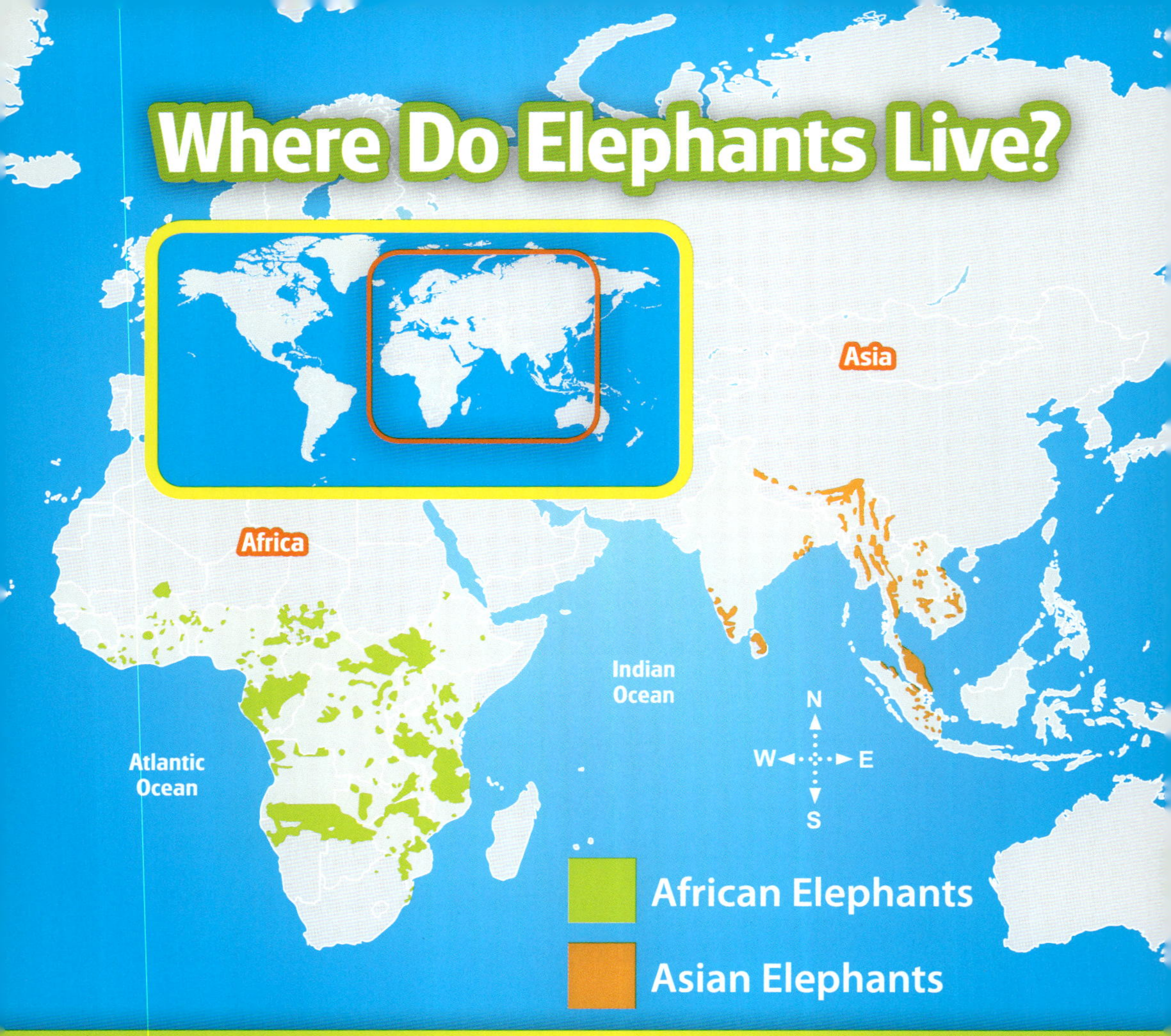

Khun is an elephant rescue worker. Many elephants need help. Asian elephants are **endangered**. Some people mistreat them. They use the elephants to make money. **Logging** elephants are forced to pull heavy loads. This wears them down. Sometimes they are injured by the extreme work. **Trekking** elephants carry people around. Saddles are put on their backs. People are lifted on.

The elephants give people a ride. Their bodies are stressed under the weight.

The calf stayed for a year. Now he's going to a nature preserve. Khun says goodbye to the calf. The Elephant Nature Park in Thailand cares for many elephants. The calf makes friends when he arrives. Then he lays down on a soft pile of sand. He smiles in his sleep.

Trekking is a popular tourist activity, but it can hurt elephants.

Laws against poaching help protect African elephants.

Khun knows it is important for people to protect elephants. Humans are their only threat. Asian elephants are threatened by big cities. New buildings and roads take over open land. The elephants have to find a new place to roam for food.

African elephants are **vulnerable**. **Poaching** threatens many African elephants. People illegally hunt them for their tusks. They use the tusks to make ivory objects. Ivory demand was high in the 1970s and 1980s. By 1990, almost half the population of African elephants was killed. Elephant populations are slowly recovering. Many countries made laws against poaching. Elephants are in the hearts of many people like Khun. They know these creatures deserve protection.

Poachers hunt elephants for their ivory tusks.

BEYOND THE BOOK

After reading the book, it's time to think about what you learned. Try the following exercises to jumpstart your ideas.

THINK

DIFFERENT SOURCES. Think about what types of sources you could find about elephants. What could you find in an encyclopedia? What could you learn at a zoo? How could each of the sources be useful in its own way?

CREATE

PRIMARY SOURCES. A primary source is an original document, photograph, or interview. Make a list of primary sources you might be able to find about elephants. What new information might you learn from these sources?

SHARE

WHAT'S YOUR OPINION? Hunting elephants is illegal in many countries. But some people think the laws should be changed. They think it should be legal for people to responsibly hunt elephants. Do you agree or disagree? Use evidence from the text to support your answer. Share your position and evidence with a friend. Does your friend agree with you?

GROW

REAL-LIFE RESEARCH. Think about what kinds of places you could visit to learn more about elephants. What other topics could you explore there?

RESEARCH NINJA

Visit www.ninjaresearcher.com/0028 to learn how to take your research skills and book report writing to the next level!

RESEARCH

DIGITAL LITERACY TOOLS

SEARCH LIKE A PRO
Learn about how to use search engines to find useful websites.

FACT OR FAKE?
Discover how you can tell a trusted website from an untrustworthy resource.

TEXT DETECTIVE
Explore how to zero in on the information you need most.

SHOW YOUR WORK
Research responsibly—learn how to cite sources.

WRITE

GET TO THE POINT
Learn how to express your main ideas.

PLAN OF ATTACK
Learn prewriting exercises and create an outline.

DOWNLOADABLE REPORT FORMS

Further Resources

BOOKS

Blewett, Ashlee Brown. *Mission: Elephant Rescue.* National Geographic Society, 2014.

Murray, Julie. *Elephants.* Abdo Publishing, 2012.

Schuh, Mari C. *The Supersmart Elephant.* Lerner Publications, 2018.

WEBSITES

FACTSURFER

Factsurfer.com gives you a safe, fun way to find more information.

1. Go to www.factsurfer.com.
2. Enter "Elephants" into the search box and click .
3. Select your book cover to see a list of related websites.

Glossary

calf: A calf is a baby elephant. An elephant calf stays with its mother for many years after it's born.

endangered: A species is endangered when its population in the wild is very low. Asian elephants are endangered.

logging: Logging is clearing and moving trees for lumber. Elephants are used by logging companies to pull logs on land or through water.

poaching: Poaching is hunting illegally. African elephants are in danger of poaching for their tusks.

roams: When an animal roams, it travels from place to place. An elephant roams to find food.

sensitive: Noticing small changes or details is being sensitive. An elephant's trunk is sensitive so it can feel or pick up small objects.

trekking: Trekking is riding elephants. Elephant trekking is a popular activity for tourists in Thailand, but it can hurt elephants.

trunk: A trunk is the part of an elephant's face that is a combination of nose and upper lip. Elephants use their trunks for eating, bathing, and more.

vulnerable: Animals are vulnerable when they are in danger of being hurt. African elephants are vulnerable from poaching.

Index

PHOTO CREDITS

The images in this book are reproduced through the courtesy of: Johan Swanepoel/Shutterstock Images, front cover; Susan Schmitz/Shutterstock Images, p. 3; Maksym Gorpenyuk/Shutterstock Images, pp. 4–5; Dmytro Gilitukha/Shutterstock Images, p. 6; evantravels/Shutterstock Images, p. 8; backpacker79/Shutterstock Images, pp. 8–9; Johan W. Elzenga/Shutterstock Images, p. 10; Jonathan Pledger/Shutterstock Images, p. 12; huang jenhung/Shutterstock Images, pp. 12–13; Talvi/Shutterstock Images, p. 14; Four Oaks/Shutterstock Images, p. 15; Mohamed El Hebeishy/Shutterstock Images, pp. 16–17; Naoto Shinkai/Shutterstock Images, p. 18 (Asian elephant); Chipmunk131/Shutterstock Images, pp. 18–19 (person); Kletr/Shutterstock Images, p. 19 (African elephant); Dawid Fourie Photography/Shutterstock Images, p. 20; Steve Bower/Shutterstock Images, pp. 20–21; Gregory Zamell/Shutterstock Images, p. 22; Chathip Suwanthong/Shutterstock Images, pp. 22–23; Red Line Editorial, p. 24; Thitisan/Shutterstock Images, p. 25; Michael Wick/Shutterstock Images, p. 26; Svetlana Foote/Shutterstock Images, p. 27; Nadezhda Bolotina/Shutterstock Images, p. 30.

ABOUT THE AUTHOR

Emma Huddleston has written books about science, sports, animals, and more. She thinks animals are fascinating. When she isn't writing, she enjoys reading and swing dancing. She lives in the Twin Cities with her husband.